inside

ABOUT ME
Start off by focusing on who you are, what you think about school and how you rate your learning skills.

Getting started
Getting down to it
Getting some answers

ATTITUDE
Work out why school is important and how to make the most of your education.

Getting there
Getting your thinking cap on
Getting clued up
Getting that feeling
Getting to grips
Getting it across
Getting down
Getting noticed

LEARNING
Make a plan to develop your skills for learning in the classroom and utilise your other talents and abilities.

Getting it straight
Getting organised
Getting it all in
Getting under control
Getting ready
Getting wise
Getting it right
Getting on

DISTRACTIONS
Identify what distractions you face and come up with strategies to deal with them.

Getting the idea
Getting your head down

RULES
Judge how rules affect you and how well you can follow them.

Getting focused
Getting done
Getting in line

HOMEWORK
Think about how you approach homework, the space and time you set aside for it and things you might improve.

Getting worked up
Getting real
Jo & Joey
Getting the message

THE FUTURE
Decide how the future might look for you.

Getting ahead
Getting a helping hand
Getting a job
Getting the picture

RECORD
Keep a record of your achievements.

Getting better
Getting it down
Hurrah

getting started

me

me...

Name:

Age:

Birthday:

Ambition:

Things I'm good at:

Things I'd like to improve at:

ABOUT ME

my best...

Food:

Book:

Friend:

Music:

Hobby:

Subject:

Other things I like:

my worst...

Nightmare:

Memory:

Phobia:

Subject:

Food:

Habit:

Other things I dislike:

note

Have a go at filling in the boxes to record all about you!

stuff

getting down to it

ABOUT ME

Discuss your responses with a friend or adult.

	yep	sort of	nope

myself

- Can you give three reasons why it's good to be you?
- Can you say something that you are good at and explain why?
- Can you say something that you are not so good at and explain why?

skills

- Can you describe (or show) how you'd let your teacher know you are listening?
- Do you believe you work hard and are achieving your full potential?
- Can you explain what things distract you from your class work and how you could prevent or deal with them?

rules

- Can you think of three school rules and say why each one is important?
- Can you state one school rule you agree with and why and one you would change and why?
- Do you think you are good at following school rules?

	yep	sort of	nope
interests			
Do you have a hobby or special interest that you spend time on?	☐	☐	☐
Can you explain how you balance your school work with your other interests?	☐	☐	☐
Can you switch easily between working alone and working with others?	☐	☐	☐
homework			
Can you explain what you could do if you got stuck on your homework?	☐	☐	☐
Do you have a tidy and quiet space at home with all the equipment you need to work on your homework?	☐	☐	☐
Do you hand in your homework regularly?	☐	☐	☐
attitude			
Can you think of three reasons why you should come to school?	☐	☐	☐
Can you imagine and describe what your future might be like?	☐	☐	☐
Would you say that you handle disappointment appropriately?	☐	☐	☐

ABOUT ME

getting some answers

What do you think?
Write your responses!

If school could only teach one subject, I think it should be

> If I was my teacher, I'd like

My teacher thinks I am

> I think my teacher is

A good teacher is someone who

> What I like about my classroom is

What I dislike about my classroom is

> We wear school uniform because

I wish there was a school club for

> Break and lunchtime at school are

My attendance at school is

My school is helping me to

I get to school by

My parent(s)/carer(s) think school is

When I'm older, my parent(s)/carer(s) think I should be a

The best school trip was

A difficulty I have overcome at school is

The most embarrassing thing that's happened to me at school is

My best tip for homework is

My earliest memory of school is when

A friend I have made at school is

I am most proud of

> ATTITUDE

getting there

Are you getting the most out of school?

Mark your answers on a scale of 1–5.
1 = Strongly Agree!
5 = Strongly Disagree!

When you've finished, add up the numbers you circled and read about your score below.

1	2	3	4	5	I make use of my strengths at school.
1	2	3	4	5	I have good friendships with peers.
1	2	3	4	5	I travel to/from school with ease.
1	2	3	4	5	I think my teacher cares about me.
1	2	3	4	5	I enjoy break and lunchtime.
1	2	3	4	5	My attendance is good.
1	2	3	4	5	I regularly complete my homework.
1	2	3	4	5	I am a member of a school club/team.
1	2	3	4	5	My work seems at the right level for me.
1	2	3	4	5	There are lots of things to do at school.
1	2	3	4	5	I usually keep out of trouble.
1	2	3	4	5	I wear my uniform without much complaint.
1	2	3	4	5	I feel safe at school.
1	2	3	4	5	I can concentrate at school.
1	2	3	4	5	I'm happy with my achievements at school.
1	2	3	4	5	I take part in extra-curricular opportunities and trips whenever I can.

TOTAL:

16–37
You do your best to take advantage of the opportunities your school offers you. You'll have a strong CV in the future which will help you get further in education and land a good job you'll enjoy. Keep going and do everyone proud!

38–58
You find school has a fairly even balance of positives and negatives. Find out what else is on offer at school to fire up your enthusiasm, like joining a new club. Look closely at the things you dislike most and talk about how you could change them.

59–80
If there's something you're worried or fed up about, talk to an adult at home or school right now as they can help improve the situation. Do your best to take part in a bit more and see how well you could do with some extra effort – don't let down the future you.

ATTITUDE

getting your thinking cap on

What do you think about the stuff schools teach?
Some subjects might be more important than you think!
Try thinking of which subject(s) could help you...

save someone's life

stay healthy and live longer

keep in touch with someone far away

mend broken objects

find a place without using a 'sat nav'

order dinner on a holiday abroad

work out how much less you'll pay in a '30% off' sale

understand how to wash your new jacket

Think of something you have learnt today.

When or where else could you use what you have learnt?

getting clued up

ATTITUDE

The lessons you're learning at school right now are the stepping stones to your future career.

Let's think about some different jobs that people do...

Which subjects might they need to know about to do their job well?

What might happen if this person doesn't pay attention in their lessons?

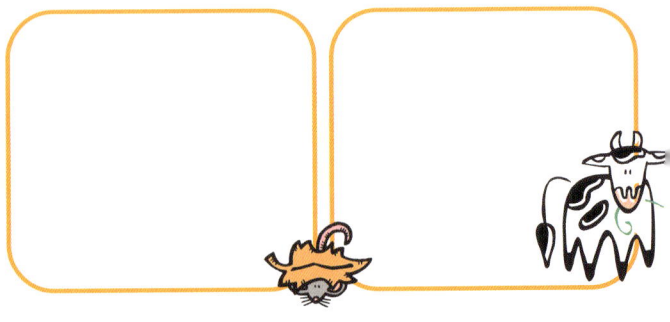

Teacher

Vet

Footballer

Nurse

Hair-Dresser

Post Man or Woman

What job do you think you might like to do in the future?

All subjects will be important to you but which subjects might be especially important for this job?

ATTITUDE

getting that feeling

Want to find your passion?

What other people most often praise or compliment me for:

What other people most often ask for my help with:

What I would do if there were no barriers or obstacles:

What I feel very strongly about:

The best experience I have had so far in my life:

What I most like to do in my spare time:

Identifying your strengths and interests can help you decide what you might like to do as a job in the future!

getting to grips

ATTITUDE

Think of some of the adults and pupils at school.
What jobs do they do?

- Midday supervisor
  ↓
  - Organising lunchtime
  - Helping in the playground

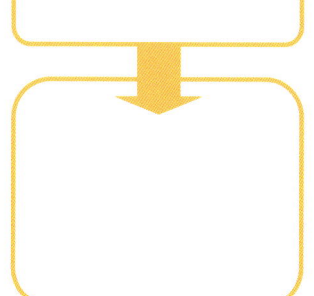

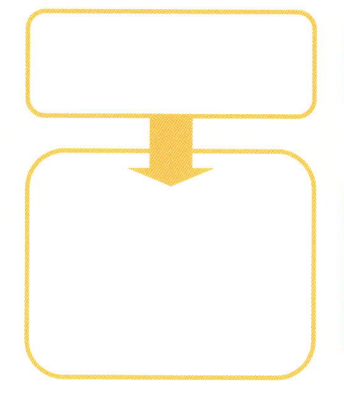

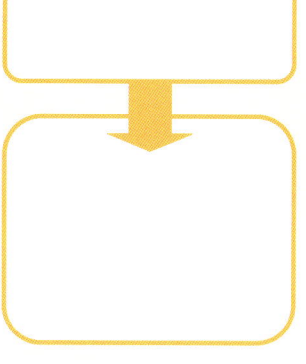

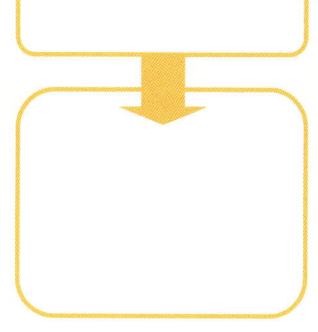

What about you?

What are your responsibilities at school?

getting it across

ATTITUDE

Things aren't always as straight forward as they first seem.
What do you think about these scenarios?

Elijah
is having difficulty completing his homework so his mum says she'll help him out. She ends up doing most of it for him because he still doesn't really understand.

Elijah should tell his teacher his mum helped him.

Strongly Agree · Agree · Not Sure · Disagree · Strongly Disagree

Why?

Olivia
forgot to learn the spellings she was set for homework. She's worried her teacher will tell her off. During the test she realises she can see her friend's answers so she copies them.

Olivia should copy just this once.

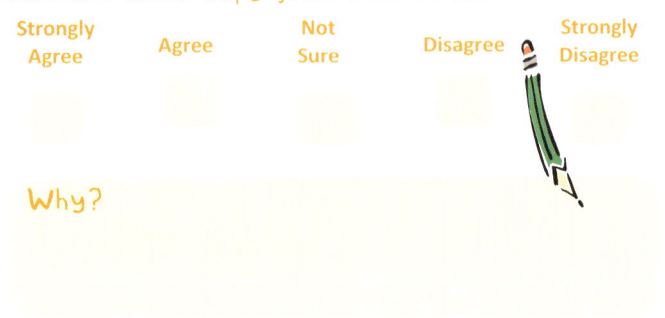

Strongly Agree · Agree · Not Sure · Disagree · Strongly Disagree

Why?

Ben
and his classmates take a test which will help the teacher decide which Maths set they'll be in. Ben helps his best friend in the test so that they'll be put into the same set.

Ben should help his friend in the Maths test.

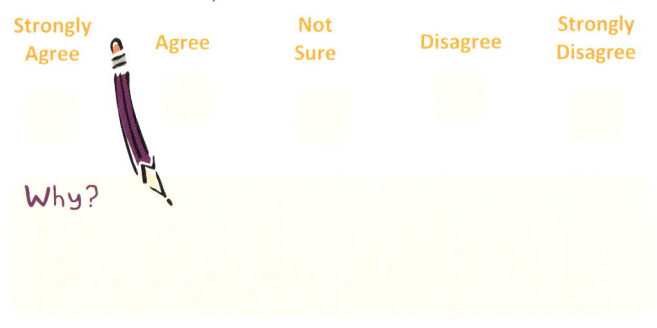

Strongly Agree · Agree · Not Sure · Disagree · Strongly Disagree

Why?

Harpreet

really doesn't enjoy school but loves to read and do work at home. She rarely attends school but is doing quite well in most of her work.

Harpreet should stay at home to work.

Strongly Agree | Agree | Not Sure | Disagree | Strongly Disagree

Why?

Laura

is a very talented gymnast and spends each evening training. Her trainer thinks she even has a chance to compete at the Olympics. She gets tired and won't do her homework.

Laura should focus on her gymnastics.

Strongly Agree | Agree | Not Sure | Disagree | Strongly Disagree

Why?

Nate

gets detention for something he didn't do. He protects his friend, Ian, who is the true culprit so that Ian can go to a football game he's saved up to go to the same evening.

Nate should keep quiet this time.

Strongly Agree | Agree | Not Sure | Disagree | Strongly Disagree

Why?

Write about a time at school when you had to make a hard decision...

getting down

ATTITUDE

How do you deal with disappointment when you don't do as well as you hoped?

Disappointment is

I felt really disappointed when

What helped me to feel better was

People might feel disappointed in me when

Somebody disappointed me when

Some **inappropriate** ways to deal with disappointment:

Some **appropriate** ways to deal with disappointment:

Top Tips

★ Concentrate on your goal, not on the disappointment, anger or frustration of the setback. Blaming others or being a 'sore loser' won't help.

Don't be embarrassed by a setback, we all experience them.

What do we mean by 'positive thinking'?

All of these pupils are disappointed. Each pupil handles this feeling in a different way but is it appropriate or inappropriate?

"I can't believe you won! It's not fair! I bet you cheated! I worked much harder than him, Miss Smith!"

Why?   Appropriate or Inappropriate?

"I missed a goal again! I'm not playing anymore. I'm totally rubbish. The team will never win any matches with me in it. I'm no good."

Why?   Appropriate or Inappropriate?

"Well done! What a beautiful painting! You deserved to win the competition! How does it feel to win? Can you teach me some of your techniques?"

Why?   Appropriate or Inappropriate?

A 'good winner' must handle *other people's* disappointment. Be kind and tell others they did well too.

Often, we can learn from a setback. Think about what didn't go right and come up with a plan to avoid the same mistakes.

Discuss how these pupils might all have reacted differently.

getting noticed

ATTITUDE

Think of people, both famous and non-famous, who you admire. How do these people influence you?

Who do you admire?	Why?	What does this show you?
My Granddad	Because he decided to learn a new language so he could live abroad.	That it's never too late to learn new skills and to keep practising until you're perfect.

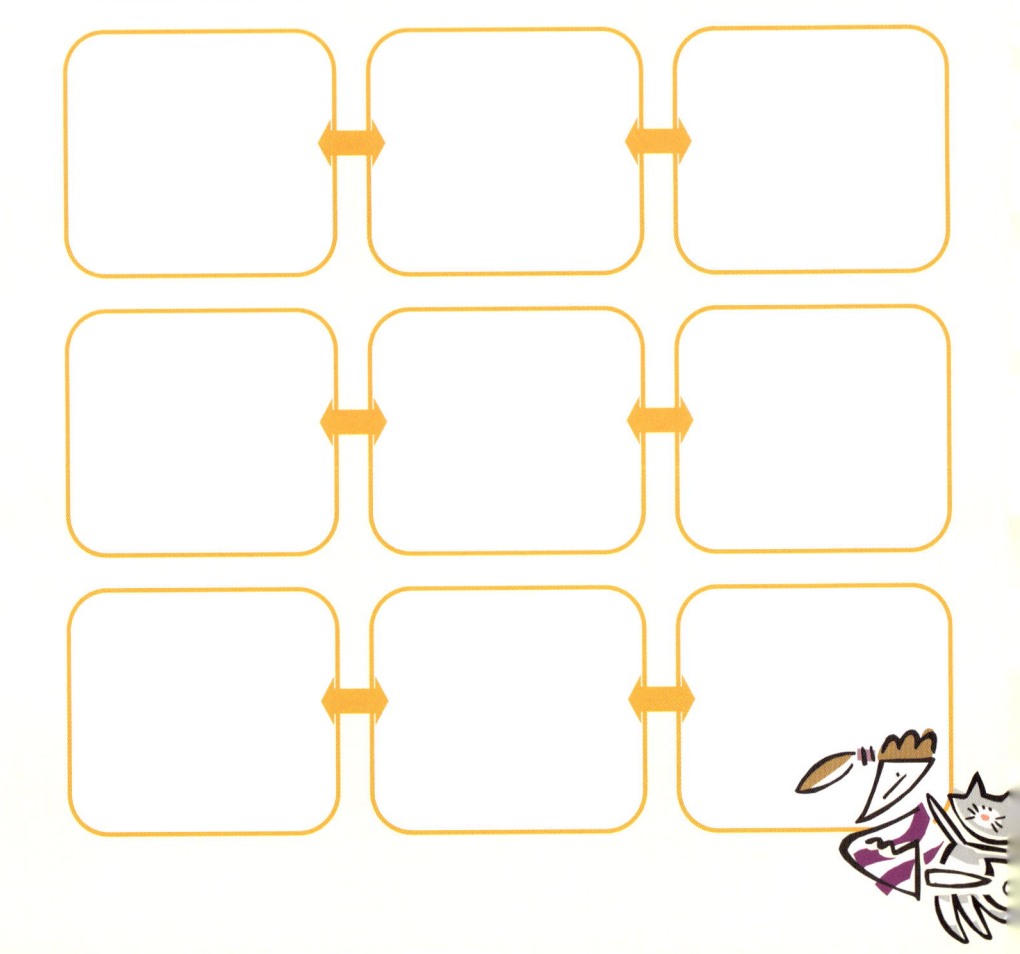

Why might people admire you?

What does this show others?

What personal qualities do you think all these people needed to achieve their goals?

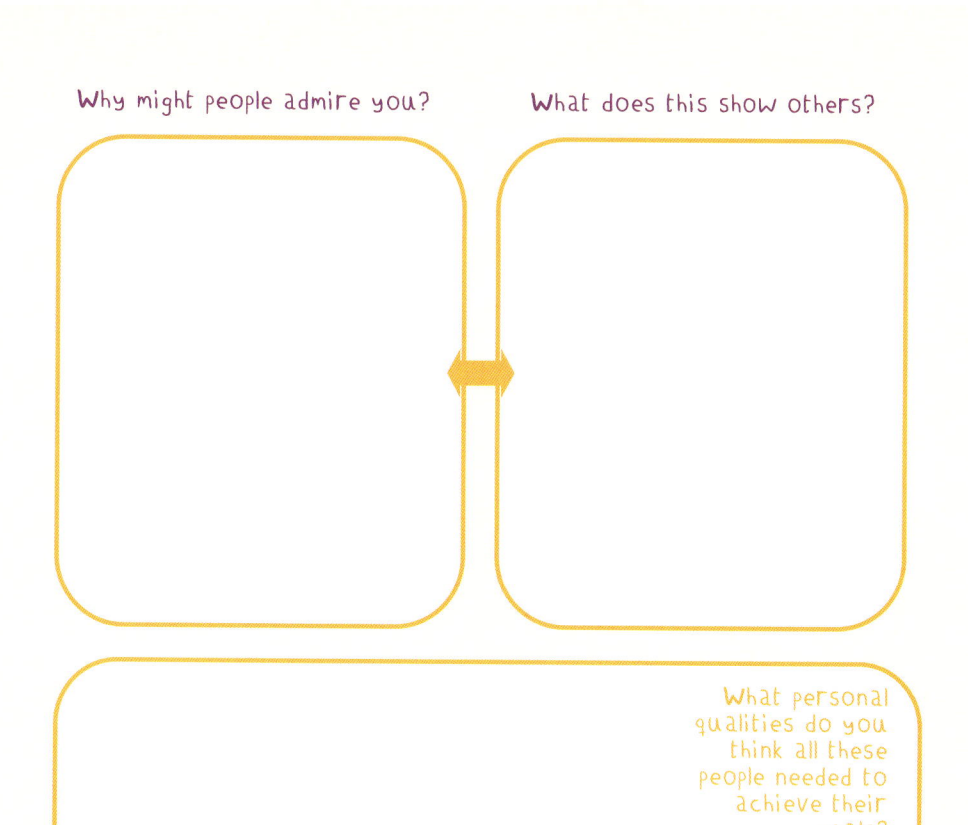

What personal qualities do you think you need to achieve your goals?

getting it straight

LEARNING

What do you think about school?

Things I am good at:

Things I'd like to improve at:

What I like best about school:

What I like least about school:

I learn best when:

I'm bored when:

I come to school for:

School would be better for me if:

As Head Teacher, I would:

getting organised

LEARNING

How organised are you?

In the morning before school, do you wake up to:

- ★ the sound of your alarm clock which you set the night before
- ★ the sound of your family getting up- it's usually about the right time
- ★ your mum yelling at you to get up or else you'll be late again

Your first lesson of the day is P.E. You:

- ★ get changed quickly and start warming up
- ★ change into your stinky kit which hasn't been washed for a while
- ★ have to sit and watch because you forgot your kit

You are a member of a lunchtime club. You:

- ★ check your watch and turn up five minutes early
- ★ wait for midday supervisors to remind you and turn up just in time
- ★ were too busy with your mates, you missed the club altogether

You have some homework to complete. You:

- ★ write it in your homework diary, do it and hand it in on time
- ★ write it on scrap paper, do it, then hand it in a day late
- ★ forget to write it down, forget to do it, forget to hand it in

You've been invited to a party. You:

- ★ turn up on time together with a present and card
- ★ call your friend to check where it is because you lost the invitation
- ★ forget

★ **Mostly Green**
Super organised!
You're usually on time
and in the right place!
Well done!

★ **Mostly Orange**
Need to improve!
Write a 'To Do' list then
decide which jobs are most
important and do them first!

★ **Mostly Purple**
Disorganised!
Use a diary and a watch!
Tidy up your desk/room/bag so
you know where things are!

getting it all in

LEARNING

Be prepared to get organised!
What might these people need to pack in their bags?

Preston's Bag
School day trip to the seaside

Preston might need:

Jo's Bag
Shopping in town with her sister

Jo might need:

Sean's Bag
His dad's house overnight

Sean might need:

How can you tell that someone is organised?

Rita might need:

Rita's Bag

Camping for a weekend

Joey might need:

Joey's Bag

The park with friends

Your Bag

Going to school... what items will you need every day?

getting it under control

LEARNING

Write down which subjects you have on each day!

Write down what you will need on each day!

Monday

Tuesday

Wednesday

Thursday

Friday

Use this chart as a reminder when packing your bag (the night before)!

LEARNING

getting ready

Ready to test your memory?

The aim of this game is to see how many items you can remember without looking!

Give yourself one minute to memorise the items!

Tip:
Try picturing each object with a person you know!
(Granny scared of the mouse...)

Tip:
Try creating a silly story linking all the items in some way!
(Michael the mouse lived in a shell...)

Tip:
Try putting a tune, rhythm or even just funny sounds to each item!
(Snip! Scissors!)

Now you can use these tips to remember other things too such as friends' birthdays, spellings, or items on a shopping list!

getting wise

LEARNING

Try this quiz to discover your preferred learning style!

1. In a lesson, I prefer the teacher to:

- Do a demonstration
- Write or draw on the board
- Talk about the subject

2. I follow instructions best when:

- Someone tells me
- Someone shows me
- They are written

3. In my spare time, I enjoy:

- Watching TV
- Listening to music
- Playing a game

4. After meeting someone, I am most likely to remember:

- What they were doing
- What they looked like
- What they were saying

5. If I could choose, I'd rather take part in:

- A Music lesson
- An Art lesson
- A P.E. lesson

6. I most enjoy stories when:

- I act it out
- Someone reads it aloud
- I read it myself

Mostly SEE — A 'visual learner' likes to observe and see things written or printed in books or on the board. This learner likes colour, lists, charts and diagrams.
TIP: Make sure you can see the board.

Mostly HEAR — An 'auditory learner' likes listening, enjoys discussions and talking things through and remembers verbal instructions best.
TIP: Ask questions if you need to.

Mostly DO — A 'kinaesthetic learner' likes to be active, use their hands, go exploring, try things out and can put things together easily.
TIP: Make use of equipment.

getting it right

LEARNING

If learning was a recipe, what ingredients would it contain?

effort

getting on

LEARNING

Are you an effective learner?

1. Ready to work?

Follow this check list for 5 tasks and see how ready you are to start learning.

	TASK 1	TASK 2	TASK 3	TASK 4	TASK 5
Are you listening carefully?	☐	☐	☐	☐	☐
Are you sitting where you should be?	☐	☐	☐	☐	☐
Do you know what you've got to do?	☐	☐	☐	☐	☐
Are you ignoring distractions?	☐	☐	☐	☐	☐
Do you have everything you need?	☐	☐	☐	☐	☐
Are you following class rules?	☐	☐	☐	☐	☐

before

2. Stuck on your work?

Follow this check list for 5 tasks and see how you handle getting stuck.

	TASK 1	TASK 2	TASK 3	TASK 4	TASK 5
Have you tried to apply what you know?	☐	☐	☐	☐	☐
Have you asked a buddy (if allowed)?	☐	☐	☐	☐	☐
Have you looked back at previous work?	☐	☐	☐	☐	☐
Have you tried revisiting it at the end?	☐	☐	☐	☐	☐
Have you re-read the instructions/work?	☐	☐	☐	☐	☐
Have you asked your teacher?	☐	☐	☐	☐	☐

during

3. Checked your work?

Follow this check list for 5 tasks and see how you could improve the quality.

	TASK 1	TASK 2	TASK 3	TASK 4	TASK 5
Have you checked it makes sense?	☐	☐	☐	☐	☐
Have you corrected spelling mistakes?	☐	☐	☐	☐	☐
Have you corrected punctuation errors?	☐	☐	☐	☐	☐
Have you shown your knowledge?	☐	☐	☐	☐	☐
Have you answered everything?	☐	☐	☐	☐	☐
Do you feel you've tried your best?	☐	☐	☐	☐	☐

after

What do we mean by an 'independent learner'?

DISTRACTIONS

getting the idea

How would you deal with these distractions?

Your neighbours want you to come out to play but you've got homework to do!

A boy behind you in class keeps kicking you whilst you are working!

You are in assembly and your friend wants to tell you about her holiday!

You had a bad night's sleep and are worrying about what's going on at home.

How might your actions distract others?

DISTRACTIONS

getting your head down

How much time do you lose to distractions?
Tick the boxes for the distractions which regularly affect you.

A People Distractions

- [ ] Worrying about *someone*
- [ ] Annoying classmate
- [ ] Classroom interruptions
- [ ] Afraid of the teacher
- [ ] Chatting to your friends

B Work Distractions

- [ ] Worrying about *class work*
- [ ] Too many/too few tasks
- [ ] Work is too easy/too hard
- [ ] Equipment
- [ ] Disinterest in the task

C Environmental Distractions

- [ ] Worrying about *something*
- [ ] Arrangement or comfort of seating
- [ ] Noise
- [ ] Day-dreaming
- [ ] Hunger/thirst/ needing the toilet

Which distraction has the biggest negative impact on your concentration at school?

What can you do to reduce this distraction?

Remember, you can choose how you respond to a distraction!

getting focused

RULES

What is acceptable behaviour in your classroom?

If I finish my work early, I should...

If I don't feel very well, I should...

If I need to go to the toilet during a lesson, I should...

If I need help with my classwork, I should...

If I have problems with someone on my table, I should...

If I have forgotten to bring something I need to school, I should...

What else does your teacher expect you to do?

If I...

getting done

RULES

If you broke these rules, what consequences would you face at your school?

Being late:

Bullying in the playground:

Talking when you shouldn't be:

Not using the lollipop person to cross the road:

Do you think these punishments are fair?

Chewing gum in class:

Not doing or not handing in your homework:

Copying someone else's work:

Not playing by the rules in a game:

Stealing:

Why do you think we need rules and punishments?

getting in line

RULES

Pretend that you are the new Head Teacher and imagine that you are changing the rules in your school!

Which rules do you agree with?

Rule:

Why?

Rule:

Why?

Rule:

Why?

Which rules do you disagree with?

Rule:

Why?

Rule:

Why?

Which rules would you add?

Rule:

Why?

Rule:

Why?

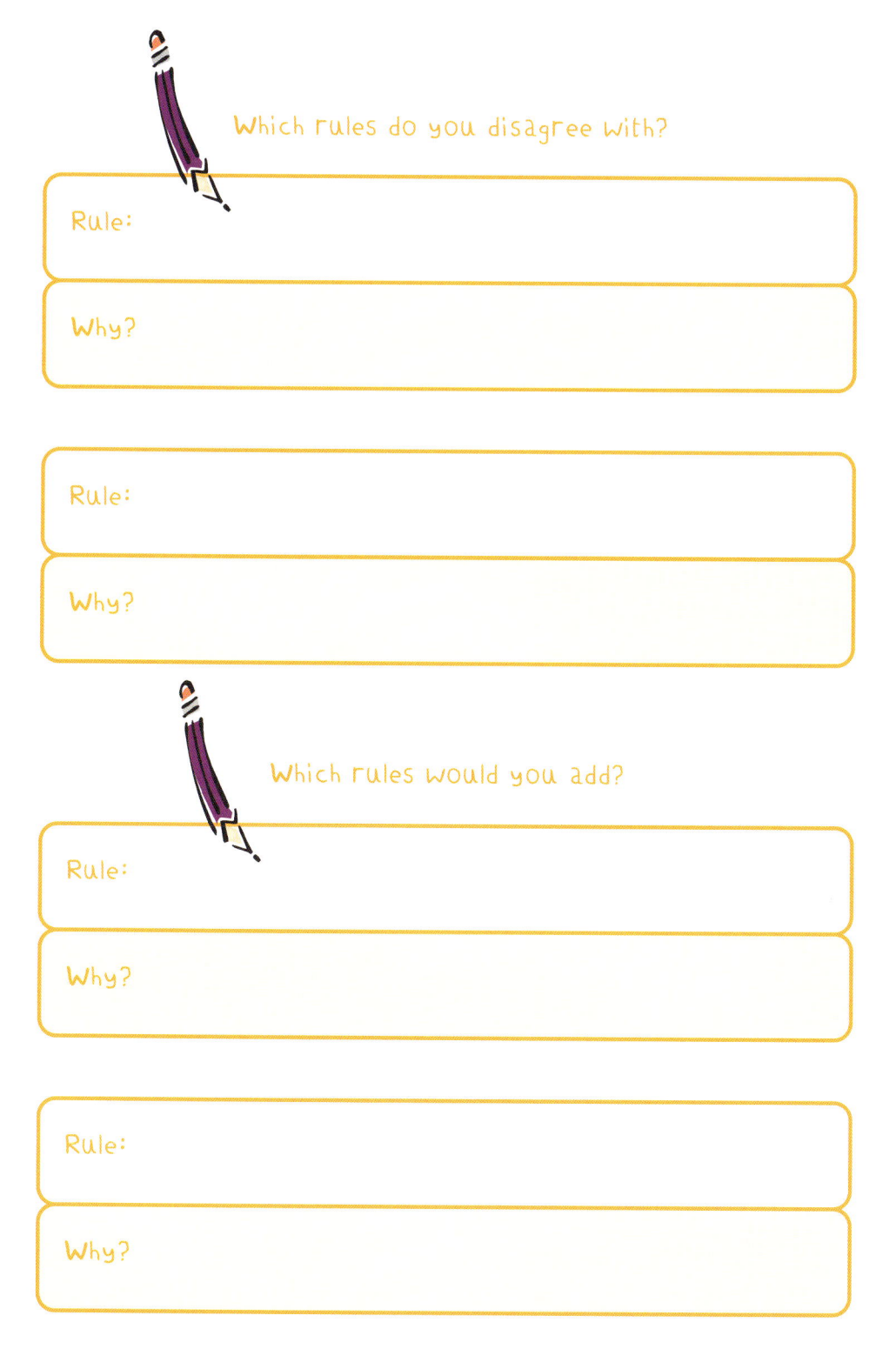

getting worked up

HOME WORK

Think about your homework!

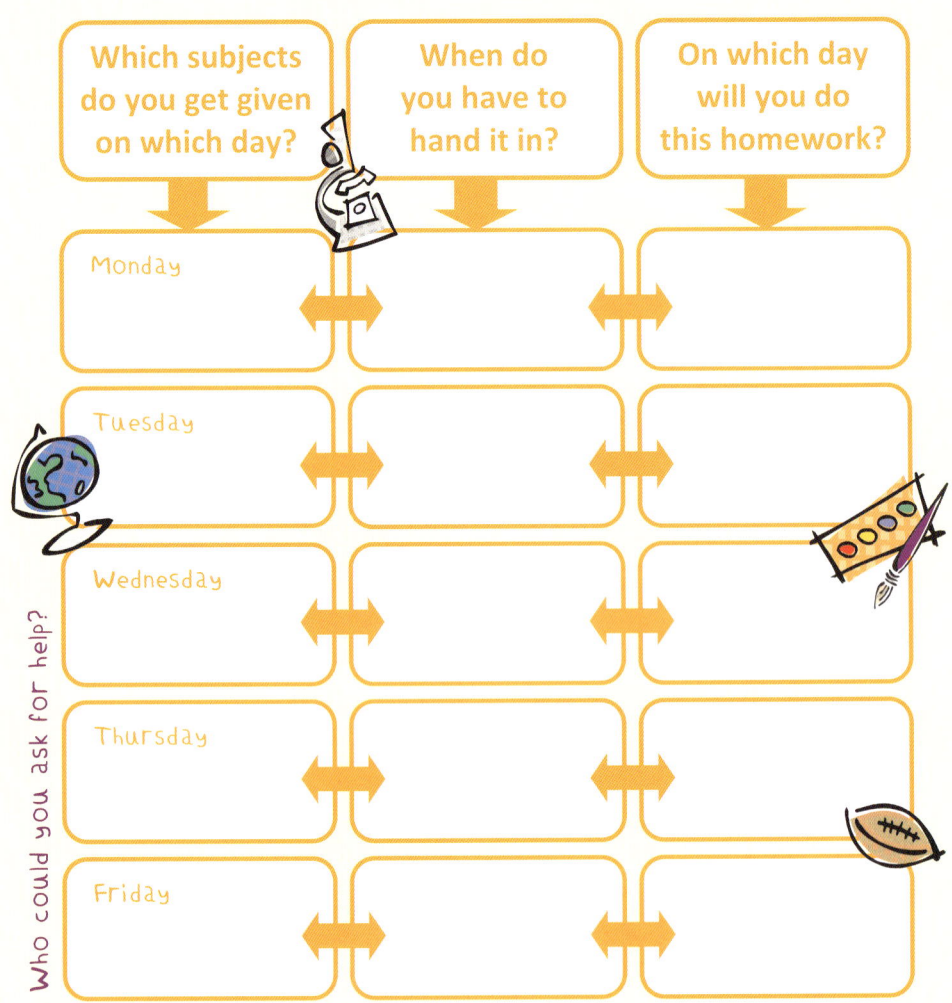

Which subjects do you get given on which day?	When do you have to hand it in?	On which day will you do this homework?
Monday		
Tuesday		
Wednesday		
Thursday		
Friday		

Who could you ask for help?

Leaving homework until the last minute can make you feel stressed which means you're more likely to make mistakes!

'Take five' if you need to re-energise!

Reward yourself when it's done!

Work in a quiet, tidy, comfy space!

Cheating by copying someone else's homework won't help you improve!

Does your school have a homework club you could try out?

getting real

HOME WORK

For your next piece of homework, record how it went using this page and discuss it with an adult at school or home.

Subject:

Have I got all the equipment I need? ☐

Have I got a tidy, quiet space to work in? ☐

Do I feel physically ready to work? ☐
(Not hungry, thirsty or needing the toilet)

Time started work:

Time finished work:

Break taken:

Help needed:

Distractions/interruptions I had to overcome:

How I felt about this homework:

Handed in? ☐ On time? ☐ Discussed with an adult? ☐

HOME WORK

Jo & Joey

Here's a common situation...

Jo: Hey Joey! What's up?

Joey: Sob! Sniff! I can't do my homework!

Jo: Huh? Why not?

Joey: It's too hard! I'm really worried!

Jo: Can't you ask your mum for help?

Joey: I did but she works it out a different way to how Miss Smith showed us!

Jo: Well, what about telling Miss Smith the dog ate your work?

Joey: No, I can't lie! She might ask me to do it again and then what would I say? I'm scared she'll be cross...

Jo: Oh Joey!

What advice could Jo give Joey?

Why do you think this?

HOME WORK

getting the message

There are lots of different types of thinking. Write down a time when you had to use each of these types of thinking.

Planning   Memorising

Creating   Problem-Solving

Reflecting

What others can you think of?

FUTURE

getting ahead

How do you imagine your future?

To be

To have

I would like...

To find out

To learn

To see

To know

To remember

getting a helping hand

FUTURE

Write down five things that you will need to do so that you can achieve your dreams...

Action Point 1:

Action Point 2:

Action Point 3:

Action Point 4:

Action Point 5:

Your future is in your hands!

FUTURE

getting a job

Use this application form to apply to your teacher for a job in your classroom.

Application Form

Name

Position Applied For

Skills

Top Tip
SKILLS: What qualifications or strong abilities do you have that would be useful in this job?

EXAMPLE: If you're applying for a library monitor job, you might be able to write that you are at a high reading level at school (if it's true)! You can explain that this means you'll know about different types of books.

How can you make your application form stand out?

Experience

Top Tip
EXPERIENCE: What things have you done in the past that would help you perform this job well?

EXAMPLE: If you're applying for a plant watering job, you might be able to write that you are a keen gardener at home (if it's true)! You can explain that this would help you to know how much water to give certain plants.

How would you fit this job into your school day?

Top Tip

HOURS: When do you think you can do this job? On a real application form, it might ask you how many hours you can do each week.

EXAMPLE: If you're applying for a tidying job in your classroom, you could write that you'd spend 10 minutes on this every lunchtime.

Personal Statement

Why is it important to write neatly?

Top Tip

STATEMENT: Why do you want this job? How will it help you to develop your skills even further?

This is often one of the most important parts of an application form because it helps the employer (your teacher, in this case) to get a sense of your personality.

EXAMPLE: If you're applying for a job as a litter monitor, you might be able to write about how much you love animals (if it's true!) and want to protect them from the harm that litter can cause.

Achievements & Hobbies

Top Tip

HOBBIES: What do you enjoy doing in your own time?

EXAMPLE: You can write anything here as this is your chance to show a little more about who you are. Your hobbies don't always have to be relevant to the job you're applying for but sometimes it helps.

When is the deadline for your application?

Good Luck!

getting the picture

FUTURE

Draw a picture to show how you see yourself in the future!

In this picture, I am...

getting better

RECORD

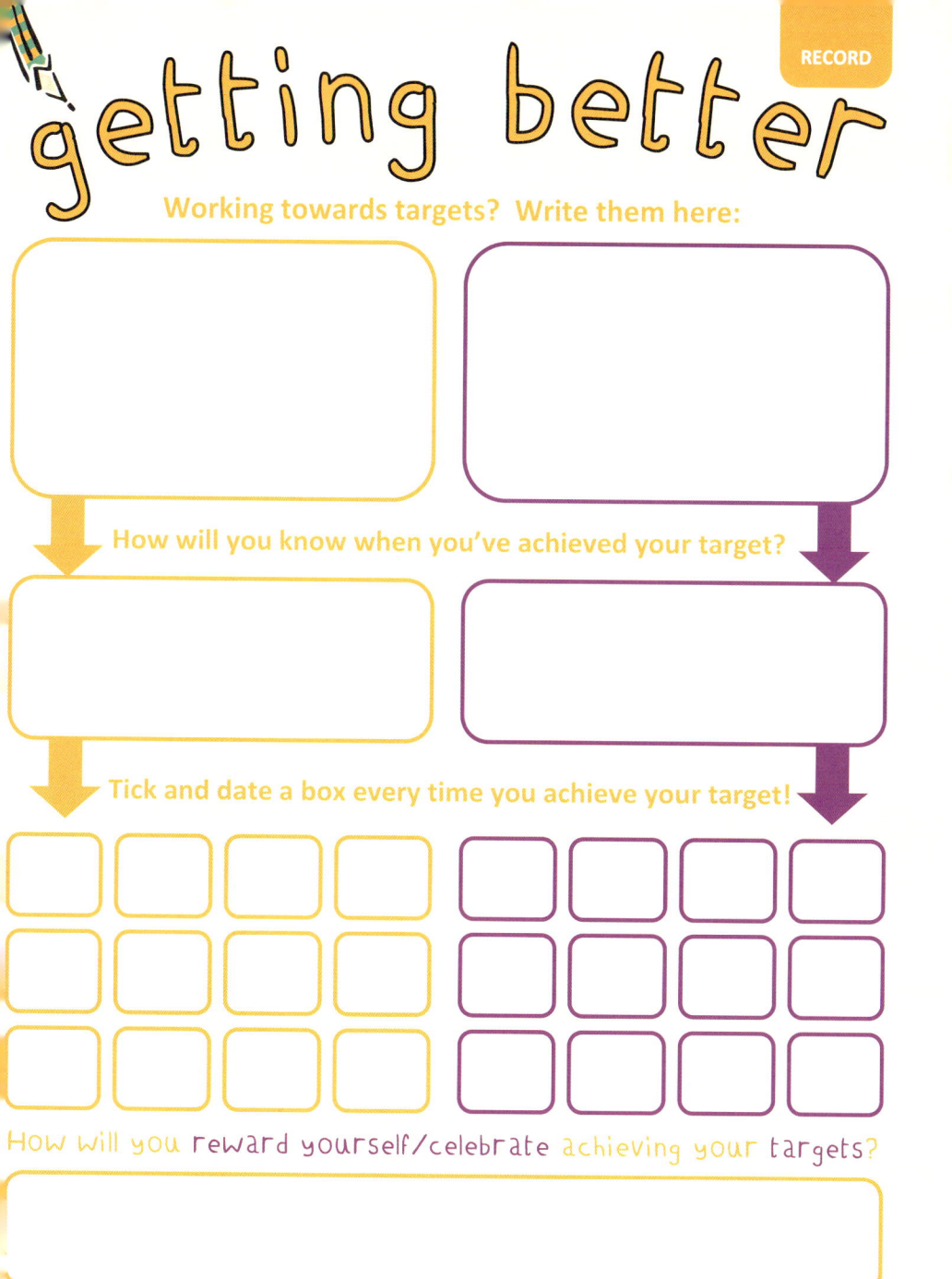

Working towards targets? Write them here:

How will you know when you've achieved your target?

Tick and date a box every time you achieve your target!

How will you reward yourself/celebrate achieving your targets?

Are your targets SMART?

* Specific * Measurable * Achievable * Relevant * Time Limited

getting it down

RECORD

Record your learning achievements here.

Did you do better in a spelling test
or did you reach the end of a book?

Date

Date

Date

Date

Date

Date

Date

Which achievement are you most proud of and why?

RECORD

hurrah

You've completed 'Achieving And Attaining'!

What have you learnt about yourself?

What have you learnt about others?

What advice would you give others like you?

What positive change will you start making to your life today?

How would you describe the 'new' you?